IT'S ALL ABOUT YOU & ME BABY

ABOUT THIS JOURNAL

Do you remember the first time you met the love of your life?

Your first impressions?

Your first kiss?

How about your first date?

This fill-in-the-blank journal is designed to help you relive those adorable memories, and more.

You'll share your stories, dreams, thoughts and feelings about the sweet, funny, quirky, cute (and not so cute) things you've experienced as a couple.

There are over 50 heartwarming prompt questions and conversation starters in this journal. One to be answered by you, and the other by your partner.

Although the questions are the same, you'll each have your own interpretation of events. That's what will make completing this journal extra fun.

You can answer a question a day, randomly pick a question per week, or whip right through the whole thing in one sitting.

There are no hard or fast rules about how this 'works'.

By the end of this journal, you'll have a keepsake memory book filled with stories, and facts about your life, as well as a deeper insight and appreciation for your relationship.

Fill out your details on the next page.

There's even space to add a photo or draw a picture of the two of you... if that's your thing.

Whether you choose to keep these memories to yourselves or, pass them down to future generations, that's totally up to you.

Enjoy!

THIS JOURNAL BELONGS TO:

———————— & ————————

WE'VE BEEN TOGETHER FOR

————————————————

THIS IS US

♥ YOU ♥

THE FIRST TIME I NOTICED YOU

_____

_____

_____

♥ ME ♥

THE FIRST TIME I NOTICED YOU

_____

_____

_____

♥ YOU ♥

WHERE AND WHEN WE FIRST MET
(AS IN WE ACTUALLY SPOKE TO EACH OTHER)

_____

THIS IS HOW I REMEMBER
OUR FIRST MEETING

_____
_____
_____
_____
_____
_____

♥ ME ♥

WHERE AND WHEN WE FIRST MET
(AS IN WE ACTUALLY SPOKE TO EACH OTHER)

_____

THIS IS HOW I REMEMBER
OUR FIRST MEETING

_____
_____
_____
_____
_____
_____
_____

♥ YOU ♥

THE FIRST THING YOU SAID TO ME

_____

_____

_____

♥ ME ♥

THE FIRST THING YOU SAID TO ME

_____

_____

_____

♥ YOU ♥

MY FIRST IMPRESSION OF YOU

_____

_____

_____

♥ ME ♥

MY FIRST IMPRESSION OF YOU

_____

_____

_____

❤ YOU ❤

ON OUR FIRST DATE WE WENT TO

_____

AND YOU WERE WEARING

_____

♥ ME ♥

ON OUR FIRST DATE WE WENT TO

_____

AND YOU WERE WEARING

_____

♥ YOU ♥

OUR FIRST DATE IN ONE WORD

_____

♥ ME ♥

OUR FIRST DATE IN ONE WORD

_____

♥ YOU ♥

'OUR SONG' IS

_____

WHENEVER I HEAR IT I

_____

_____

_____

♥ ME ♥

'OUR SONG' IS

_____

WHENEVER I HEAR IT I

_____

_____

_____

♥ YOU ♥

WE HAD OUR FIRST KISS ON

———————— AT ————————

AND IT WAS

_____

♥ ME ♥

WE HAD OUR FIRST KISS ON

_____ AT _____

AND IT WAS

_____

〜〜〜 ♥ 〜〜〜

♥ YOU ♥

WHO SAID THE 'L' WORD FIRST

♥ ME ♥

WHO SAID THE 'L' WORD FIRST

_____

♥ YOU ♥

HOW I FELT AFTER SAYING
THE 'L' WORD FOR THE FIRST TIME

_____

_____

_____

♥ ME ♥

HOW I FELT AFTER SAYING
THE 'L' WORD FOR THE FIRST TIME

_____

_____

_____

♥ YOU ♥

THE FIRST PERSON YOU TOLD ABOUT US

_____

_____

_____

♥ ME ♥

THE FIRST PERSON YOU TOLD ABOUT US

♥ YOU ♥

THE MOMENT I KNEW YOU WERE THE ONE WAS WHEN

_____

_____

_____

WE MADE THINGS OFFICIAL BY

_____

ON THIS DATE

_____

♥ ME ♥

THE MOMENT I KNEW YOU WERE THE ONE WAS WHEN

_____

_____

_____

WE MADE THINGS OFFICIAL BY

_____

ON THIS DATE

_____

♥ YOU ♥

THE FIRST TIME YOU COOKED FOR ME

_____

MY HONEST OPINION

_____

_____

_____

♥ ME ♥

THE FIRST TIME YOU COOKED FOR ME

_____

MY HONEST OPINION

_____

_____

_____

♥ YOU ♥

THE THING I FIND MOST
ATTRACTIVE ABOUT YOU

_____

_____

_____

♥ ME ♥

THE THING I FIND MOST ATTRACTIVE ABOUT YOU

_____

_____

_____

♥ YOU ♥

OUR MOST ROMANTIC DATE

_____

_____

_____

♥ ME ♥

OUR MOST ROMANTIC DATE

_____

_____

_____

♥ YOU ♥

OUR FUNNIEST DATE

_____

_____

_____

♥ ME ♥

OUR FUNNIEST DATE

_____

_____

_____

♥ YOU ♥

OUR WORST DATE

_____

_____

_____

♥ ME ♥

OUR WORST DATE

_____

_____

_____

❤ YOU ❤

THE BEST GIFT YOU HAVE GIVEN ME TO DATE

_____

_____

_____

♥ ME ♥

THE BEST GIFT YOU HAVE GIVEN ME TO DATE

_____

_____

_____

♥ YOU ♥

THREE WORDS I WOULD USE
TO DESCRIBE YOU

_____

_____

_____

♥ ME ♥

THREE WORDS I WOULD USE
TO DESCRIBE YOU

_____

_____

_____

♥ YOU ♥

I FIRST MET YOUR FAMILY ON

_____

WE WERE AT

_____

THIS IS HOW I REMEMBER THE EVENT

_____

_____

_____

♥ ME ♥

I FIRST MET YOUR FAMILY ON

_____

WE WERE AT

_____

THIS IS HOW I REMEMBER THE EVENT

_____

_____

_____

♥ YOU ♥

THE MOST UNUSUAL MEMBER OF YOUR FAMILY

_____

_____

_____

♥ ME ♥

THE MOST UNUSUAL MEMBER OF YOUR FAMILY

_____

_____

_____

♥ YOU ♥

OUR FIRST ROAD TRIP

_____

_____

_____

♥ ME ♥

OUR FIRST ROAD TRIP

_____

_____

_____

♥ YOU ♥

A MEMORY FROM A WEDDING OR PARTY WE ATTENDED AS A COUPLE

(IF MARRIED, SHARE A MOMENT FROM YOUR WEDDING)

_____

_____

_____

♥ ME ♥

A MEMORY FROM A WEDDING OR PARTY WE ATTENDED AS A COUPLE

(IF MARRIED, SHARE A MOMENT FROM YOUR WEDDING)

_____

_____

_____

♥ YOU ♥

THE CUTEST THING ABOUT YOU

_____

_____

_____

♥ ME ♥

THE CUTEST THING ABOUT YOU

_____

_____

_____

♥ YOU ♥

THE FIRST TIME I SAW YOU CRY

_____

_____

_____

♥ ME ♥

THE FIRST TIME I SAW YOU CRY

_____

_____

_____

♥ YOU ♥

YOU MAKE ME A BETTER
PERSON BECAUSE

_____

_____

_____

♥ ME ♥

YOU MAKE ME A BETTER
PERSON BECAUSE

_____

_____

_____

♥ YOU ♥

THE MOST ROMANTIC THING
YOU'VE EVER DONE

_____

_____

_____

♥ ME ♥

THE MOST ROMANTIC THING YOU'VE EVER DONE

_____

_____

_____

♥ YOU ♥

YOUR NICKNAME FOR ME

_____

♥ ME ♥

YOUR NICKNAME FOR ME

_____

♥ YOU ♥

OUR FIRST FIGHT

_____

_____

_____

HOW WE MADE UP AFTERWARDS

_____

_____

_____

♥ ME ♥

OUR FIRST FIGHT

_____

_____

_____

HOW WE MADE UP AFTERWARDS

_____

_____

_____

♥ YOU ♥

THE THING I LOVE THE MOST ABOUT US

_____

❧ ♥ ❧

♥ ME ♥

THE THING I LOVE THE MOST
ABOUT US

♥ YOU ♥

YOUR MOST ANNOYING HABIT

_____

♥ ME ♥

YOUR MOST ANNOYING HABIT

♥ YOU ♥

ONE THING WE DISAGREE ON

_____

♥ ME ♥

ONE THING WE DISAGREE ON

♥ YOU ♥

ONE THING I MISS MOST ABOUT YOU WHEN WE'RE APART

_____

♥ ME ♥

ONE THING I MISS MOST ABOUT YOU WHEN WE'RE APART

♥ YOU ♥

ONE WORD THAT DESCRIBES YOU FIRST THING IN THE MORNING

_____

♥ ME ♥

ONE WORD THAT DESCRIBES YOU FIRST THING IN THE MORNING

♥ YOU ♥

THE MOST EMBARRASSING THING YOU'VE EVER DONE OR SAID IN FRONT OF ME

_____

_____

_____

♥ ME ♥

THE MOST EMBARRASSING THING YOU'VE EVER DONE OR SAID IN FRONT OF ME

_____

_____

_____

♥ YOU ♥

WHO'S THE DOMINANT ONE?

♥ ME ♥

WHO'S THE DOMINANT ONE?

———————————————————————

♥ YOU ♥

YOU'RE REALLY GOOD AT

_____

_____

_____

♥ ME ♥

YOU'RE REALLY GOOD AT

_____

_____

_____

♥ YOU ♥

YOU'RE NOT SO GOOD AT

_____

_____

_____

♥ ME ♥

YOU'RE NOT SO GOOD AT

_____

_____

_____

♥ YOU ♥

YOU HAVE A WEIRD OBSESSION WITH

_____

_____

_____

♥ ME ♥

YOU HAVE A WEIRD OBSESSION WITH

_____

_____

_____

♥ YOU ♥

THE WORD, PHRASE OR SENTENCE YOU SAY REPEATEDLY

_____

_____

_____

♥ ME ♥

THE WORD, PHRASE OR SENTENCE YOU SAY REPEATEDLY

_____

_____

_____

♥ YOU ♥

THE MOST MEMORABLE EXPERIENCE
I'VE HAD WITH YOU

_____

_____

_____

♥ ME ♥

THE MOST MEMORABLE EXPERIENCE
I'VE HAD WITH YOU

_____

_____

_____

♥ YOU ♥

I HAVE NEVER PROPERLY THANKED YOU FOR

_____

_____

_____

♥ ME ♥

I HAVE NEVER PROPERLY
THANKED YOU FOR

_____

_____

_____

♥ YOU ♥

IF I WON $100,000 I WOULD SPEND IT ON

_____

_____

_____

❦

♥ ME ♥

IF I WON $100,000
I WOULD SPEND IT ON

_____

_____

_____

♥ YOU ♥

I LOVE IT WHEN YOU

_____

_____

_____

♥ ME ♥

I LOVE IT WHEN YOU

_____

_____

_____

♥ YOU ♥

IF YOU COULD CHANGE ONE THING ABOUT ME, WHAT WOULD IT BE?

_____

♥ ME ♥

IF YOU COULD CHANGE ONE THING ABOUT ME, WHAT WOULD IT BE?

♥ YOU ♥

ONE DAY I WOULD LIKE US TO

_____

_____

_____

♥ ME ♥

ONE DAY I WOULD LIKE US TO

_____

_____

_____

♥ YOU ♥

_____

MAKES ME FEEL LOVED

♥ ME ♥

MAKES ME FEEL LOVED

♥ YOU ♥

THE BEST DECISION WE'VE MADE AS A COUPLE SO FAR

_____

_____

_____

♥ ME ♥

THE BEST DECISION WE'VE MADE AS A COUPLE SO FAR

_____

_____

_____

♥ YOU ♥

I'M MOST HAPPIEST WHEN

_____

_____

_____

♥ ME ♥

I'M MOST HAPPIEST WHEN

_____

_____

_____

♥ YOU ♥

A TIME YOU MADE ME SMILE OR LAUGH SO MUCH MY CHEEKS HURT

_____

_____

_____

♥ ME ♥

A TIME YOU MADE ME SMILE OR LAUGH SO MUCH MY CHEEKS HURT

_____

_____

_____

♥ YOU ♥

YOU ARE MY

_____

♥ ME ♥

YOU ARE MY

_____

REMEMBER WHEN

FUN TIMES

YOU'RE SO CRAZY

LOVE YOU

Made in the USA
Coppell, TX
26 December 2019

13764584R00066